The Other Side Of Me

Jazmine Droste

BookLeaf Publishing

The Other Side Of Me © 2023 Jazmine Droste

All rights reserved.

No part of this publication may be reproduced, stored in a retrieval system, or transmitted, in any form or by any means, electronic, mechanical, photocopying, recording or otherwise, without the prior written permission of the presenters.

Jazmine Droste asserts the moral right to be identified as author of this work.

Presentation by *BookLeaf Publishing*

Web: www.bookleafpub.com

E-mail: info@bookleafpub.com

ISBN: 9789357740579

First edition 2023

All rights reserved.

This book is dedicated to a lot of people that have inspired me, pushed me, prayed for me, looked out for me, and never left my side. My mom (Paula Weber), for helping me become stronger by pushing me to always do my best. My brother (Dukeoda Droste) for being an amazing big brother, and always having my back no matter what. My son (Finnic Blu) for being my on hand all time best friend, giving me love, and never forgetting to tell me how much you love me. Last but NEVER least, to the many others in my life at this current time of 2023, you know who you are :), Thank you for being a part if my life. Through the good and the bad. Thank you for holding me, seeing me, speaking to me, and simply for loving me. I couldn't be here without any of you. To many to name.

ACKNOWLEDGEMENT

Dear Finnic Blu,
I hope one day you come across this book and you discover my poetry when you are feeling lonely. I promise you mom is always here and I love you forever and always. To the moon and back.

PREFACE

If you choose to read this book, I shall warn you it may get intense. Most of these invents in this book really occurred. The feelings I may express may seem like a lot. I have manic Bi-Polar, manic Depressive, PTSD, and severe anxiety recently diagnosed with gastris to add to the list. I had a rough childhood. It's hard to just explain the things that I have been through but poetry helps me express the pain of it all. My grandfather and my mother both enjoy writing very much so I'd like to think that's where my heart emerged from. I started writing when I was only a meer 8 years old and have never given up the passion.

Mini Me

You have me tied around your fingers.
You are my whole entire world.
At the beginning it was so scary.
We've come 4 years now.
You are learning and growing so fast.
I wish I had more time to last.
Everyday is a new adventure,
With different paths to choose,
Different ways to go,
And new things around each corner.
It's going to be hard.
It's going to be scary.
It's going to be fun.
It's going to be amazing.
Take a deep breath,
Look at the world.
Take One step and a time.
You are the world.
Take on the world.
I'm so glad you are my mini me.

I Love You

Turn out the lights.
Take a breath.
Lay down our heads.
Sometimes we sleep,
Sometimes we play.
Sometimes we fight
In the end,
Of all the days.
However they start
To however they end,
I'm glad I have you here.
I don't know what else to say,
Besides...
I love you.

Be Strong

I know this is hard.
I know you are sad.
I know you are mad.
Broken, and hurt.
Left in the dirt.
I know you are afraid,
And torn down.
But please
Be strong.

Blessed

Even when you weren't here,
You still knew everything.
I zipped up the bag of memories,
Stuffed it in a safe,
Put the safe 6ft under,
And threw the key in the river.
Becuse... you left
for awhile.
Had your first....
Then we found eachother again.
You introduced me to your second....
My heart was filled with joy.
Now, you a wonderful bestfriend/mom.
And becuse.
I stayed at your side
like you did mine....
Now I receive the title...
God Auntie..
I'm blessed.. simply blessed.

New Friends

Here's to new friends,
Met in old places.
Here's to meeting you..
Technically again.
Here's to the first hello,
Here's to first game we played,
Here's to yesterday's yesterday,
And hell here is to today.
Glad you came around,
Hope you stay around.
Thank you.. VERY MUCH.
for being a new uncle & new friend

Picking Favorites

The person I cry too,
The person thats NEVER left.
The person who teaches me life.
The person I never wanna loose.
You have loved me for 22 years.
You have held me,
And helped me.
You have changed me,
And showen me how to be free.
You are my rock,
You are my light,
You are my world.
You are life...
You are not just any mom...
You are the best mom.

Stolen And Afraid

Trapped in my own darkness,
Held captive by a person
Who I thought loved me.
Watching the clock tick,
Counting the tears falling
Off my face.
Stolen virginity.
Stolen heart.
Stolen bed.
Stolen person.
Stolen life.
Afraid of love.
Afraid of men.
Afraid of living.
Trapped.
Scared.
Alone.
When I was eight....
My world was taken away.

I needed you

You know the stories.
You know the truth.
You know the lies.
You have the proof.
I was broken...
And you knew.
I needed help.
I needed love.
I needed space.
I needed you.
You stuck around.
Then broke me down.
You left.
Just like the others.
I was heartbroken.
But you changed me,
For the good and the bad.
You changed me
For everything I had.
You replaced me,
With someone new.
Now it hurts to even look at you.
Thanks for being here before,
Thanks for leaving us in the dust,
This is coming from the core.

You turned my heart into a pile of rust.
Now it's even to hard to trust.
Saddned by your life,
Becuse you tried to ruin it.
In return.... we made Him.
I thought I needed you
Because boy did I
Need you....
Get it right though.
I needed you,
I don't now.
So thanks and goodbye.

I'm glad you're back

The day I met you,
Was a weird day.
So many things I wanted to say.
Instead I swelled up with jealousy.
You did not know
All the things he said.
The things he lied about,
The things... about you.
The words dug knives into the earth.
And I stupidly believed
his every single word.
That was till I finally met you.
He said you were depressed...
But you seemed so happy and blessed.
I loved seeing that side of you... I said.
Then I found out that's you everyday.
I looked at him and laughed,
because compared to me,
you were absolutely perfect.
I'm so glad after we both lost
that dirtbag
we became friends.
I'm so glad you came back around.
I mean it with all my heart.
I missed you so much.

Big Brother

You held my hand,
You treated me right.
You said you loved me,
Every single night.
When I felt alone,
You were always there.
Right across the way,
No matter the time of day.
You never left my side,
Even held me when I cried.
Thank you for being my bestfriend.
Thank you for teaching me to be me,
And always being you.
I'm so glad you're my big brother.

Battlefield

Why can't I get out if this dream?
Why is everyone yelling at me?
What did I do now?
Shit.. how do I fix this?
I'm sorry.. god I'm sorry.
I didn't mean to upset you.
I wish I had better words.
Please don't yell at me,
No don't raise your hands.
Just get out of my face,
But please stay. Don't go.
I don't know how to explain this,
I don't know if you'll understand.
I'm happy,
I'm scared.
Now I'm sad.
And I'm angry..
This is bad.
Relentless all these triggers..
Laughing in my face,
Spewing so much hate.
Help me I'm fucking scared.
I need you here.
Hold my hand,
Don't let go.

Darkness.
Bloodshot eyes,
Pain in my chest,
I can't breath.
Lost inside my own head.
Suurounded..
with all these terrible feelings.
I feel like I'm loosing the battle,
Of PTSD

Hate

You were supposed to love me.
Give me happiness and strength.
You were supposed to teach me,
What it was like to have a man.
Instead you broke me.
You left me on the side of the road,
To bleed out calling,
Pleading, begging for help.
You were supposed to teach me trust,
And guide me through this life.
Instead you ruined me,
And made me afraid.
You were supposed to love me.
Instead you made me HATE you.

Learning To Drive

One foot down.
Now breathe.
You can do this.
You can.
Slowly ease.
Don't panic.
It's ok.
We will learn this.
One step at a time.
One foot down.
Look around.
You are doing great.
Take a breath.
Now it's time,
to take another step.
You can do this.

Frustrations

The yelling and complaints..
Feeling the restraints.
I do my best and I try my best.
But what about the rest.
I'm tired and I'm sore,
What do you want me to say more?
Chin up Or chin down,
Turn around your frown.
It'll be okay.
It's just another day.
Scream and yell,
You do it so well.
Complain and fight,
It's all right.
It's just simple frustrations,
We need to let out.

My Little Love

Just take it
Take it all.
All the love I have.
All the hope I have.
Take it all away.
Throw it in the river,
With the key.
Watch it float away.
The life we once had,
Forever changed.
Change my thoughts,
My memories,
My love,
Change it all,
And take it all.
Lock it safely in your heart,
And never let go.

Don't Go

All the games you play,
All the lies you told,
Am I the pray?
This I so old.
I keep trying,
But you keep lying.
I just want to love you,
Hold you, need you, and see you.
You keep turning away.
Pushing further off my path.
I can't do the math.
I juked life and people,
Just to get to you.
And now this is where we are.
I just want to be the one,
This is not fun.
Please love me back.
Please want me back.
Please Please please
Don't leave me like everyone else.

Anxiety

Silent cries,
With no tears.
Punching pillows,
With no screams.
Waiting for someone,
For something,
To hear me.
In the darkness
Of anxiety.

Stroke of Silence

Before you touched me.
I was happy.
Before you yelled at me.
I always talked.
Before you hit me,
I always played.
Then one day,
Everything changed.
You became violent,
Relentless.
I became afraid, lost, lonely.
Every touch,
Came a tear.
Every yell,
Broke my heart.
I cried for hours,
Alone in the darkness.
Nobody to listen,
In the stroke of silence.

Help Me

Why am I such a failure?
I don't feel like a good friend.
I don't feel like a food mom.
Daughter nor girlfriend.
Everyone says that I'm amazing.
Everyone says they love me.
I believe it all,
But it's just so hard.
I wish I could be better,
Instead of this.
Wish I could be stronger,
But I feel like this.
Someone help me.

Dreams

I've dreamt of better days.
I've dreamt of better nights.
Hopeful as can be,
As I lay down to sleep.
Rest my head upon the pillow,
Eyes wide open,
Til I drift off to sleep.
I can't count sheep,
They all ran away.
I can't count down
from any number,
Because it takes to long
for my eyes to close.
So I just lay....
In the darkness,
The silence,
The shadows.
Then I just beg myself
To please
Please please
Be a good dream.

Good Luck

To ends depth of earth.
Swear on all oaths,
To God himself.
My son is the only thing
Keeping me from snapping.
I'm no longer a simple peice of wood.
There is a fire swelled under my heart.
It's burning through my entire body.
The rage is conquring me.
The happiness we once had,
Gone in the dust.
In the flames.
You should be afraid.
Very very afraid.
I will find you, and them.
You will loose this battle.
Don't look at me.
Don't speak to me.
Don't underestimate me.
You wanna play games,
Thats fine by me.
Don't you dare use my son as a pawn.
Be a man and stand up to me.
You are not ready for my storm.
You are not ready for my pain.

My fire is about to set your world in pain.
Good Luck.

www.ingramcontent.com/pod-product-compliance
Lightning Source LLC
LaVergne TN
LVHW010256210726

843508LV00020B/2787